Workplace Grace

Other Resources by Bill Peel

What God Does When Men Lead

Discover Your Destiny (coauthored with Kathy Peel)

Discover Your Destiny (eight-session video series)

Living in the Lab Without Smelling Like a Cadaver

Living in the Lions' Den Without Being Eaten

The Saline Solution (coauthored with Walt Larimore)

What God Does When Men Pray

Where Is Moses When We Need Him? (coauthored with Kathy Peel)

The Busy Couple's Guide to Sharing the Work and Joy (contributor)

Marriage and Family Resources at www.FamilyManager.com

Workplace, Evangelism, and Men's Ministry Resources at www.24SevenFaith.com

Other Resources by Walt Larimore

10 Essentials of Happy, Healthy People: Becoming and Staying Highly Healthy

God's Design for the Highly Healthy Child

God's Design for the Highly Healthy Teen

Alternative Medicine: The Christian Handbook (coauthored with Dónal O'Mathúna)

Bryson City Tales: Stories of a Doctor's First Year of Practice in the Smoky Mountains

Bryson City Seasons: More Tales of a Doctor's Practice in the Smoky Mountains

Bryson City Secrets: Even More Tales of a Small-Town Doctor in the Smoky Mountains

The Saline Solution: Sharing Christ in a Busy Practice (coauthored with Bill Peel)

Lintball Leo's Not-So-Stupid Questions About Your Body

SuperSized Kids: How to Protect Your Child from the Obesity Threat
(coauthored with Cheryl Flynt and Steve Halladay)

His Brain, Her Brain: How Divinely Designed Differences Can Strengthen Your
Marriage (coauthored with Barb Larimore)

The Honeymoon of Your Dreams: How to Plan a Romantic Life Together
(coauthored with Susan Crockett)

Why A.D.H.D. Doesn't Mean Disaster
(coauthored with Dennis Swanburg and Diane Passno)

Time Scene Investigators: The Gabon Virus (a novel)
(coauthored with Paul McCusker)

Christian Health Blog at www.DrWalt.com/blog

Christian Health Resources at www.DrWalt.com

Autographed Books available at www.DrWalt.com/books

Workplace Grace

6 Sessions

Becoming a Spiritual Influence at Work
Participant's Guide

Bill Peel & Walt Larimore
with Stephen & Amanda Sorenson

Previously titled *Going Public with Your Faith*

ZONDERVAN®

ZONDERVAN.com/
AUTHORTRACKER
follow your favorite authors

ZONDERVAN

Workplace Grace Participant's Guide
Copyright © 2006, 2010 by William Carr Peel, ThM and Walt Larimore, MD

Previously titled as *Going Public with Your Faith Participant's Guide*

Requests for information should be addressed to:

Zondervan, *Grand Rapids, Michigan 49530*

ISBN 978-0-310-32379-2

Cover design: Jody Langley
Interior design: Ben Fetterley

Printed in the United States of America

10 11 12 13 14 15 16 17 18 19 20 /DCI/ 20 19 18 17 16 15 14 13 12 11 10 9 8 7 6 5 4 3 2 1

CONTENTS

PREFACE

"I want my life to count. I don't want to look back at the end and think I wasted it."

Most of us have heard other people express this sentiment and have expressed it ourselves. Our desire to make a positive difference—to be significant—before God is a healthy desire. Those of us who are Christians often define this significance in terms of our efforts to share the gospel, to spread the Word at home and abroad so that other people come to faith in Jesus Christ.

Unfortunately, few of us have experienced much success in this area of Christian living. Our efforts to share Christ often seem uncomfortable, awkward, ineffective—perhaps even counterproductive. The formulas and methods we have learned for sharing the gospel may sound good at an evangelism seminar, but they just don't seem to work for us in the real world. Thus many of us, despite our desire to carry out our biblical responsibility, have simply given up.

If you are one of these people, we have hope and help for you! If you have questions about how to effectively share your faith, *Workplace Grace* will help. In the sessions that follow, you will learn how the seemingly insignificant words you speak and actions you take can have great significance before God and in the lives of people you encounter every day. The truth is, you can have a significant spiritual impact on the lives of the men and women with whom you work, or wherever you go.

—Bill Peel and Walt Larimore

SPIRITUAL ECONOMICS

Evangelism is not an event but a relational process, and God has gifted each of us to play a critical role in drawing men and women to himself.

BEFORE YOU BEGIN

Your experience in this session will be greatly enhanced by reading the introduction and chapter 1 of the book *Workplace Grace*.

QUESTIONS TO THINK ABOUT

1. When you hear the word *evangelism*, what thoughts, feelings, or personal experiences come to mind?

2. What is your definition of *evangelism*?

3. What do you think makes evangelism successful or unsuccessful?

4. What would grace look like in the context of your workplace?

VIDEO OUTLINE

We want our lives to count

God's distribution plan

The *process* of evangelism versus the *event* of conversion

Discovering God's job for us in the evangelism process

VIDEO DISCUSSION

1. As you watched the water cooler scenes, what did you learn about yourself and the way you go about the process of evangelism?

2. Name your colleagues you would most like to see come to Christ.

3. Walt made a clear distinction between the process of *evangelism* and the event of *conversion* when someone "prays the prayer." Why is this distinction important for us to understand?

4. Why are relationships such an important part of the evangelism process?

GROUP BIBLE EXPLORATION

EVANGELISM: GOD'S DISTRIBUTION METHOD

Of all the methods the Creator of the universe could have used to spread the gospel throughout the world, he chose to use ordinary Christians from all walks of life—the kind of men and women we meet as we go about daily life. God didn't handpick superstars to take his message to the world. Instead, he chose you and me to have a vital role in drawing spiritually needy people to himself. But how does God want us to distribute his message? What exactly is our role and what does the process look like?

> ## BE A SPIRITUAL INFLUENCE? OF COURSE YOU CAN!
>
> The greatest privilege in the world—being part of someone's journey to Jesus—can begin with something as simple as having a cup of coffee with a colleague, listening compassionately when a customer shares why she has had a rough week, or doing something beyond the call of duty for a boss or employee who's under stress.

1. The Bible provides plenty of instruction in how we are to go about being the witnesses God wants us to be in our world. Let's consider a few key Scripture passages that will help us better understand our role as God's witnesses.

   a. One day Jesus told a parable about a farmer sowing seed in different types of soil and later explained the parable to his disciples. It turns out that the parable was about evangelism—how people receive the message of his kingdom! Read Matthew 13:1–8, 18–23 and notice the emphasis Jesus places on the whole process of evangelism, not just an abundant harvest. What does Jesus' teaching reveal about people's responses to the "seed" of his Word?

b. Just as Jesus did, the apostle Paul often used an agrarian model to illustrate his teaching about evangelism. What key points do we learn about our role in the evangelism process from Paul's instruction in 1 Corinthians 3:5–9?

c. What did Jesus say to his disciples about the tasks of preparing for and reaping a spiritual harvest? (See John 4:35–38.)

Now that we have highlighted the scriptural teaching on evangelism, let's take a look at event-oriented evangelism (the method with which we may be most familiar) and consider how it differs from process-oriented evangelism.

CONTRASTING VIEWS OF EVANGELISM	
Evangelism as an Event	Evangelism as a Process
Views evangelism as a point in time when a person recites the gospel message and encourages non-Christians to "pray the prayer" and place their faith in Jesus.	Views evangelism as a process, much like farming, that cultivates hearts, plants spiritual seeds, and nurtures their growth.
Tends to focus on the actions of the person who is "witnessing." May employ standardized, assertive, and sometimes intrusive methods of pushing the conversation toward our agenda whether that is comfortable for the non-Christian or not.	Recognizes that God typically uses a number of people to draw a person toward a relationship with Jesus. Each witness in the process seeks to discover what God is doing in a person's life (God's agenda), then graciously employs his or her natural gifts and abilities to join in that effort.

Can make people apprehensive about telling others about Jesus due to fear of failure or guilt feelings if the results are minimal.	Creates joy and enthusiasm as people realize how God can use them as one link in a chain of people who help non-Christians discover Jesus and take incremental steps toward faith in him.

THE WORK AND THE RESOURCES

For many people who become Christians as adolescents or adults, the evangelism process involves significant relationships and personal interaction with Christians. Studies show that a person who comes to Christ as an adult may have nine to twenty-five such relationships. Each relationship in the chain prompts what Walt calls "many mini steps" that eventually lead to a person making a commitment of faith in Jesus Christ. Let's take a closer look at the resources we have to nurture meaningful relationships throughout the evangelism process.

2. In their book, Bill Peel and Walt Larimore describe four distinct phases of evangelism—cultivation, planting, harvesting, and multiplying. Take a few moments to familiarize yourself with each phase as highlighted in the following chart. As a group, discuss the role relationships of trust play in each phase. If time permits, read the biblical example given for each phase to gain further insight.

PHASE	FOCUS	ACTIONS REQUIRED
Cultivation	John 4:4–30 Build trust in the messenger so there will be trust in the message; display the benefits of a relationship with God	Build meaningful relationships and live in an honest, authentic way in proximity to non-Christians
Planting	Acts 8:26–39 Address intellectual barriers—misconceptions, misinformation, and ignorance about God and the Christian faith—and feed the appetite for truth	Thoughtful, patient, humble "planting" of biblical truth through our conversations and in response to questions non-Christians ask

cont.

Harvesting	Acts 26:1–29 Address the person's resistance—indecision or unwillingness—to making the decision to trust Jesus	Continued conversations, respectful persuasion, and consistent prayer
Multiplying	Acts 11:19–26 Implant new Christians into faith communities where they can grow and flourish spiritually	Provide personal care that encourages spiritual growth and development

3. Jesus referred to the cultivation process as the "hard work" of evangelism (John 4:38). For most of us, cultivation will be our primary focus, but God never gives us a job without also providing the resources we need to accomplish it. Being a pipeline of God's grace in the evangelism process truly is a privilege that every one of us can enjoy. All we need to begin is a heart that sincerely desires others to experience the fullness of God's salvation, and God will provide the resources we need.

Read each of the following Scripture passages to discover what God promises to provide. Think about how each provision will help us in the evangelism process.

a. God loves us and will protect and provide for us.

   Romans 8:31–39

   Isaiah 40:28–31

b. God gives us his Spirit and power.

   Acts 1:8

   Matthew 10:18–20; 28:19–20

c. God's power is at work on our behalf.

   Ephesians 3:20–21

d. God gives us his grace.

   Ephesians 4:7, 11–13

   2 Corinthians 9:8

BE A WITNESS? OF COURSE YOU CAN!

Solid relationships are a vital part of extending God's grace. When church growth experts Win and Charles Arn asked about fourteen thousand people, "What or who was responsible for your coming to Christ and your church?" between 75 and 90 percent responded, "A friend/relative." This leads the Arns to conclude, "Webs of common kinship (the larger family), common friendship (friends and neighbors), and common associates (work associates and people with common interests or recreational pursuits) are still the paths most people follow in becoming Christians today."

—Win and Charles Arn, *The Master's Plan for Making Disciples* (Grand Rapids: Baker, 1998) pp. 45–46

4. During this session, we have had a crash course in what for some of us is a new model for evangelism. Would anyone like to share how your thinking about evangelism has changed (or is changing)? What questions about this model of evangelism would you like to discuss?

5. In light of the biblical model for evangelism that we have explored, describe ways in which the workplace provides opportunities for ordinary people like us to effectively share God's message of grace.

DID YOU KNOW?

Researcher and futurist George Barna, author of many books including *Evangelism That Works*, reports that one out of three adults in America is unchurched and that two-thirds of these unchurched adults want to experience God in a deeper, more tangible, and significant way. This means that two out of every nine adults is unchurched and *wants* to experience God! It's been said that the United States contains the third largest unchurched population in the world!

PERSONAL JOURNEY: TO DO ON YOUR OWN BETWEEN SESSIONS

During this session, you learned about the process of evangelism and the unique role you can have in joining what God is doing in people's lives. The following exercises will enhance your understanding and application of what you have discovered during this session.

1. Think about how you became a Christian. How many people extended God's grace and helped you take small spiritual steps or shared truths about Jesus and the Bible with you before you made your decision? List each person who positively and/or negatively influenced you along your journey. Write down what was especially memorable about your interaction with that person. Take special notice of your relationship with the individuals who influenced you the most.

PERSON WHO INFLUENCED ME	WHAT MADE A DIFFERENCE

2. Take a moment to think about the daily conversations you have with people—particularly people in the workplace or people with whom you interact on a regular basis. What kinds of things are easiest for you to talk about? What kinds of things do you talk about most frequently? What characteristics and qualities of these relationships make it easy to talk on a personal level?

In what ways might these observations help you extend your influence by nurturing more significant relationships with non-Christians?

3. It is helpful to anticipate the ways in which you can intentionally extend God's grace in your workplace—or, if you work in the home or are retired, in your spheres of influence. Which of the following five evangelism models best suit your particular situation? How might you use one or more of them to effectively share your faith with the people you most care about?

Proclamational	Public preaching; announcing God's truth to a large audience.
Confrontational	Initiating a conversation with someone (often a stranger) with the aim of leading him or her to Jesus. May cause non-Christians to feel pressured to respond and may create emotional barriers. May do more harm than good if not done skillfully.
Intentional	Hosting nonthreatening events that expose friends and colleagues to Jesus in a nonreligious atmosphere. Conducted with the hope that the events will spark spiritual interest and stimulate non-Christians to want to know more about Jesus. Provides connections for the host to build on afterward.
Passive	Using symbols, objects, and/or art to arouse spiritual curiosity. Includes religious art, tracts, magazines left in waiting rooms, etc. Has the benefit of always communicating, but the values of the person using this method must match the message.
Relational	Building bridges of friendship with coworkers, family members, friends, neighbors, and associates who share common interests or recreational pursuits—and graciously telling them about Jesus. Views "successful" evangelism as a process of helping people take steps toward Jesus. This method was used during the growth of the early church.

4. If you have not already done so, make a list of the people you would love to see come to faith in Christ and begin praying for them by name. Ask God to give you natural opportunities to join him in what he is doing to draw each person to himself.

NAME	PLACE IN THEIR SPIRITUAL JOURNEY

5. For further study on the topics covered in this session, read the introduction and chapter 1 of the book *Workplace Grace* if you have not done so already.

BEFORE SESSION 2

Please read chapters 2, 7, and 12 of the book *Workplace Grace*.

CALLED TO THE WORKPLACE

Although God may and surely does call some men and women to leave the workplace for professional ministry, it is the exception. He wants Christians to go to work for the same reason they go to church: to worship God and serve their fellow humans.

BEFORE YOU BEGIN

Your experience in this session will be greatly enhanced by reading chapters 2, 7, and 12 of the book *Workplace Grace.*

QUESTIONS TO THINK ABOUT

1. Describe the mission field(s) to which God has called you. If your workplace is not on your list, why not? In what ways do you think God does or does not value your work life?

2. Do you feel you are "wasting" your time in your workplace? If so, how might this attitude be affecting your ability to be a witness there?

3. What do you have in common with other Christians in your workplace? What do you talk about when you are together? What concerns do you share with one another? What do you pray about?

VIDEO OUTLINE

Where are God's heroes?

Finding your sacred calling

Values in the workplace/valuing the workplace

Prayer and partnerships

VIDEO DISCUSSION

1. Bill makes some strong statements regarding the consequences of the church and Christians having "abandoned" the workplace because of the view that secular vocations are less valuable than those considered "sacred" vocations. What are his concerns for Christians and for the workplace? What evidence of these consequences do you see in your workplace? in your church?

2. Several people interviewed in this video shared how they "bring their faith to work." What encouragement or new ideas did they provide that you can apply in your workplace?

GROUP BIBLE EXPLORATION

THE WORKPLACE: WHERE GOD ROLLS UP HIS SLEEVES

The sacred-secular division that so many Christians have accepted as true is actually a remnant of Greek philosophy, which taught that working with your hands using physical materials was beneath the gods or men who had the means to choose how they spent their time. In contrast, the Bible considers all of life to be spiritual and leaves no room for dualistic thinking that labels some work as "sacred" and other work as "secular." God wants his followers to bring him into the workplace "where the kingdom of God most powerfully meets the kingdom of this world." He wants our workplace to be where we roll up our sleeves to accomplish his purposes.

1. Colossians 3:22–4:6 was written to slaves and masters, which for the people of Paul's day represented a situation roughly comparable to our modern employee–employer relationship. Though there are some obvious cultural differences, this passage still reveals great insight into how God wants us to view our work. Read this passage and answer the following questions:

   a. How should a Christian's faith influence his work ethic?

   b. What does God see as the real purpose and motivation for our work?

c. What kinds of work does Paul consider to be God's work (or as he says "working for the Lord")?

d. What about our work attracts others to want to know more about our faith?

GOT TEAMWORK? GOD INVENTED IT!	
God's personality demonstrates teamwork: Genesis 1:26	God himself is a unity of three persons — Jesus, God the Father, the Holy Spirit — each uniquely contributing to the work of the one God.
God thinks teamwork is a good idea for people too: Genesis 2:18	God said it wasn't good for man to be alone, so he created Eve. In fact, the Hebrew word translated *alone* in this verse carries an overtone of separation and alienation, a sense of being incomplete.
Wise King Solomon declared the value of teamwork: Ecclesiastes 4:9–12	Solomon recognized the power and encouragement in numbers. We need one another. There is far greater strength in a team than in its individual parts.
Jesus utilized teams: Luke 6:12–13; Mark 6:7	After an entire night of prayer, Jesus chose his twelve disciples. When he sent out the disciples to heal and preach, he sent them in teams of two.

2. Just as people in the workplace work in teams and form strategic alliances in order to enhance their effectiveness, Christians need to team up in order to participate effectively in the process of evangelism.

   a. What, according to Paul, has God given to each of us and why? (See Romans 12:3–8; Ephesians 4:11–13, 16.)

   b. Why did Paul caution us not to think more highly of ourselves than we ought? (See Romans 12:3.)

PRAYER IS ESSENTIAL!

What we say about God to people is only as effective as what we say about people to God.

---

3. What enabled the early church to have such a powerful impact on its world? (See Acts 2:42; 4:23–31.)

BE A WITNESS? OF COURSE YOU CAN!

On Monday morning, the church is not in your church building. It spreads out all over the community, the nation, and sometimes the world as men and women disperse to do their work. It's out there—in the office, in the classroom, at the plant—where the kingdom of God meets the kingdom of this world.

OUR HIGHEST CALLING

Many Christians today believe that vocational Christian work is our highest calling and that being a pastor or other type of ministry professional is the only work that really matters to God and his kingdom. But God calls us to do the work of his kingdom in our workplace—where most of us extended time with non-Christians. In fact, most of the men and women in the Bible whom we look up to as "heroes" worked in what we would call the secular workplace. Let's take a few minutes to explore their work and their impact for God's kingdom.

4. Read each of the following passages and note the individual's professional work and his or her impact on the surrounding culture.

BIBLE HERO	PROFESSIONAL CALLING	SPIRITUAL IMPACT
Abraham	Genesis 13:2–6	Genesis 12:2–3
Joseph	Genesis 39:2–6, 22–23; 41:39–43	Genesis 45:4–7; 47:5–6, 11–12
Daniel	Daniel 2:48–49; 5:29	Daniel 6:3–5
Nehemiah	Nehemiah 2:1–8; 4:6, 11, 15–22; 5:6–12	Nehemiah 2:5, 17–18; 8:8–12
Proverbs 31 Woman	Proverbs 31:10, 13–18, 24	Proverbs 31:20, 25–28, 30–31
Deborah	Judges 4:4–5	Judges 4:6–10, 14

BE A WITNESS? OF COURSE YOU CAN!

No matter how God chooses to use us in the workplace, we must be careful to always pursue excellence. That means giving our employers (or employees) our best. Doing anything less, even if it's doing "God's work" on company time, will undermine our influence for Jesus. We need to go to work for the same reasons we attend church: to serve God and to serve one another.

5. In their book, Bill and Walt share a powerful warning about the sacred-secular divide, written by Dorothy Sayers more than fifty years ago:

> In nothing has the church so lost her hold on reality as in her failure to understand and respect the secular vocation. She has allowed work and religion to become separate departments, and is astonished to find that, as a result, the secular work of the world is turned to purely selfish and destructive ends, and that the greater part of the world's intelligent workers have become irreligious, or at least, uninterested in religion.
>
> —Dorothy Sayers, *Creed or Chaos?*

What is your response to her assessment?

6. Deep down, do you really believe God wants to use you right where you are? Which attitudes and/or actions may be keeping you from being all God wants you to be in your workplace or from making the most of the spiritual opportunities he brings your way?

7. Discuss at least three ways you might be able to expand your influence for Christ in your workplace. Keep in mind the need to be sensitive to other people and the requirements of your work environment.

PERSONAL JOURNEY: TO DO ON YOUR OWN BETWEEN SESSIONS

During this session, you've been challenged to think about ways in which God can use you in your workplace. The following exercises will enhance your understanding and application of what you have discovered.

1. Many tend to view evangelism as "solo," not "team" work. In what ways has what you explored in this session challenged your thinking about finding and working with other Christians in the process of evangelism? About teaming up with God in prayer?

2. If you aren't already involved with a team of like-minded Christians in your workplace, perhaps it's time to build one. Here are some suggestions for building your team:

   • Identify the part you can best play, given your skills, abilities, and resources.
   • Identify the kind of team support you need.
   • Identify Christians you have met who are committed to reaching non-Christians or at least might be interested in doing so.
   • Evaluate the gifts and resources of your immediate contacts.
   • Identify those who have the skills and experience to meet the needs of the non-Christians you influence.

Potential team members:

THE POWER OF TEAMWORK

If you think you are the only Christian in your immediate workplace, you may find potential teammates among colleagues from other companies, customers, clients, service providers, pastors, community service organizations, local business leaders, and Christian professional organizations. Be careful not to violate any company policies or privacy matters as you develop these relationships, and always make sure you know your team members well before referring non-Christians to them.

3. It can be a bit daunting to know how to begin praying for someone and how to be a witness in that person's life, but the Bible gives us plenty of ideas. Take time to read and think about the following Scripture passages that reveal ways to pray for other people and for yourself.

WHAT TO PRAY ABOUT FOR OTHERS	I WILL PRAY ABOUT THIS FOR:
That God will draw them to himself (John 6:44)	
That they will seek to know God (Deuteronomy 4:29; Isaiah 55:6; Acts 17:27)	
That they would believe the Bible (Romans 10:17; 1 Thessalonians 2:13)	
That Satan will be restrained from blinding them to the truth (Matthew 13:19; 2 Corinthians 4:4)	
That the Holy Spirit will convict them of sin, righteousness, and judgment (John 16:8–13)	
That God will send other Christians into their lives to influence them toward Jesus (Matthew 9:37–38)	
That they will believe in Jesus as their Savior (John 1:12; 5:24)	
That they will turn from sin (Acts 3:19; 17:30–31)	
That they will yield their lives to follow Jesus (Mark 8:34–37; Romans 12:1–2; 2 Corinthians 5:14–17; Philippians 3:7–8)	

That they will take root and grow in Jesus (Colossians 2:6 – 7)	
That they will become a positive influence for Jesus in their realm of influence (2 Timothy 2:2)	

WHAT TO PRAY ABOUT CONCERNING MYSELF	MY SPECIFIC NEED
That I will do excellent work that attracts others' attention (Proverbs 22:29)	
That my work will bring glory to God (Matthew 5:16)	
That I will treat people fairly (Proverbs 1:1 – 3; Colossians 4:1)	
That I will have a good reputation with non-Christians (1 Thessalonians 4:11 – 12)	
That others will see Jesus in me (Philippians 2:12 – 16)	
That my life will make my faith attractive (Titus 2:6 – 10)	
That my conversations will be wise, sensitive, grace filled, and enticing (Ephesians 4:29; Colossians 4:5 – 6)	
That I will be bold and fearless (Ephesians 6:19)	
That I will be alert to open spiritual doors (Colossians 4:3)	
That I will be able to clearly articulate the gospel (Colossians 4:4)	
That God will expand my influence (1 Chronicles 4:10)	

4. For further study on the topics covered in this session, read chapters 2, 7, and 12 of the book *Workplace Grace* if you haven't done so already.

BEFORE SESSION 3

Please read chapters 3 and 8 of the book *Workplace Grace*.

IS ANYBODY HUNGRY?

People are looking for answers to their spiritual questions from sources other than the church and Christianity.... Sadly, it will never occur to many people that Christianity has significant answers for their struggles unless someone *shows* them differently.... Don't miss the fact that *what people want, Jesus has to offer.*

BEFORE YOU BEGIN

Your experience in this session will be greatly enhanced by reading chapters 3 and 8 of the book *Workplace Grace*.

QUESTIONS TO THINK ABOUT

1. Many people today are searching for something more meaningful than more possessions, healthier bodies, and more leisure time. What are the non-Christians you know searching for? What do they really feel they are missing in life?

2. On a scale of one to ten, with one being the least, how biblically literate do you think most people are? What do you think the average person-on-the-street knows about the Bible? about Christ?

3. What misconceptions have you discovered when you have talked with people about what the Bible says?

VIDEO OUTLINE

People *are* hungry for God

Most people don't know the Bible; they don't know it is relevant

Meaningful relationships: bridges to the heart

VIDEO DISCUSSION

1. At the beginning of the video, Bill described a time when he made a casual reference to God and the woman he was speaking to was so hungry she "pulled the gospel out of me." What about Bill's approach do you think may have caused her to respond as she did? If you have had a similar experience, please share it with the group.

2. Why do you think Akin, who talks to coworkers about Christ while golfing, connects so well with them?

3. Do you agree with Bill that fewer people today are concerned about whether or not Christianity is true? Explain your response.

Modernism and Postmodernism: A Brief Summary

People in the workplace, especially Americans born after 1960, are increasingly "postmodern" rather than "modern" in their outlook on life. This shift in perspective has changed what is valuable or important to people, which requires a change in how we communicate the gospel.

For example, a modern perspective values truth and reason, whereas a postmodern perspective believes there is no such thing as absolute truth, no clear line between right and wrong. From a postmodern perspective, people who claim the Bible is "the truth" are arrogant, unintelligent, and intolerant. So if we want to communicate effectively, we must be aware of these fundamental differences in beliefs and values.

Modernism	Postmodernism
Effects have causes	"Stuff happens"
Truth is attainable	Nothing can be proven
Truth is discovered	"Truth" is constructed
Reason is trusted	Objective reason is denied
Facts are valued	Relationships are valued
Man is a biological machine	Man is a social being
Materialistic	Looking for meaning

GROUP BIBLE EXPLORATION

UNDERSTANDING SPIRITUAL HUNGER TODAY

In their book, Bill and Walt write, "At first glance, many people in our culture seem to be totally put off by religion.... But dig a little deeper, and you'll often discover that God is at work, preparing their hearts for your influence." But we cannot uncover the depth of a person's spiritual hunger until we get to know that person. We cannot communicate the gospel effectively until we discover what is personally meaningful to someone else.

1. The apostle Paul was an expert when it came to discovering what was meaningful to his audience and using that knowledge to communicate the gospel in a powerful way. In business terms, he knew how to "market" the gospel. Let's look at the apostle Paul's "marketing philosophy" at work in the city of Athens, as described in Acts 17:16–23.

    a. As Paul waited for his companions in Athens, what distressed him and how did he respond? (See vv. 16–17.)

    b. What resulted from Paul's discussions? (See vv. 18–20.)

    c. What do we know Paul learned about the Athenians—their lifestyle, their spiritual perceptions—that he used to communicate to them in a meaningful way? (See vv. 21–23.)

2. Just as every business must understand its customers, we Christians need to understand the people with whom we want to share God's grace. Using the chart below, let's consider the worldview and spiritual perceptions shared by many people in our world and talk about how the influence of these perspectives affects how we share the gospel.

Today's Perceptions	Consequences for Sharing Our Faith
Growing ethnic diversity has brought religious diversity and the perception that all religions are equally valid; personal relevance is what matters.	
Many people believe there is no such thing as absolute truth, and they view Christians as being intent on imposing their rigid rules on everyone else.	
Tolerance is the cardinal virtue. Alternative views of sexuality and lifestyle need to be accepted as valid in the culture.	
Many people are interested in spirituality but are biblically ignorant. They long for meaning but don't bother to look for it in the Bible.	
People have lost their sense of purpose, which leads to despair, cynicism, and apathy.	
People view the church as irrelevant, boring, and/or negative.	

BUILDING BRIDGES THROUGH SINCERE RELATIONSHIPS

To open ourselves up to the kind of personal observation of our lives that non-Christians need, we must intentionally spend meaningful time with them. As sincere and caring relationships develop, meaningful conversations will take place, providing a means through which biblical truth can be graciously shared. Let's look at what the Bible teaches about getting close and personal, starting with the way Jesus modeled "close-impact" evangelism.

3. How far was Jesus willing to go to establish a relationship with us? (See Luke 3:23; Hebrews 2:14, 17–18.)

4. The Gospels tell the story of Jesus' relationships with people on earth. We know that Jesus focused on building significant relationships with his disciples; we see him visiting in people's homes; we see crowds coming to see him; we catch glimpses of his friendships and close social relationships. The following Scripture passages give us insight into why and how Jesus related to people who were spiritually hungry. Discuss the implications of these examples for our relationships with non-Christians.

a. Matthew 9:10–13

b. Matthew 8:1–3

c. Luke 19:1–10

d. John 3:1–18

5. Though Jesus tailored his words to each individual he met, he always: (1) loved and repected them; (2) started where they were and used everyday stories with them; (3) talked about heaven or the kingdom of God; (4) asked questions; (5) planted seeds and gave them time and space to work things out for themselves; (6) knew when to stop talking; and (7) knew how to make them hungry or thirsty for more. How could you apply Jesus' model to your workplace?

BE A WITNESS? OF COURSE YOU CAN!

Showing grace in the workplace is not about techniques, systems, or method; it's not about overwork, but an overflow from a life in which God is actively at work. But to open yourself up to the kind of personal observation of your life that people need, you must intentionally spend meaningful time with non-Christians.

---

6. Why is finding common ground with non-Christians such an effective way to build relationships with them? What are some areas of common ground on which you have built such relationships?

7. If our faith is authentic and attractive, non-Christians will want to spend time with us and will invite us into their world—a world filled with actions, activities, and conversations that are at times offensive to God. The Bible clearly teaches us to pursue godliness and to flee evil, but we know that Jesus wants us to associate with sinners, like he did, in order to have the opportunity to share his love and truth with them.

So how do we find the balance? How do we pursue godliness in an atmosphere of evil? Is there ever a time when we need to distance ourselves from non-Christians? What precautions do we need to take when we befriend non-Christians?

DID YOU KNOW?

Despite 320,000 churches, 800,000 ordained ministers, 5,000 evangelistic parachurch organizations, Christian television and radio broadcasts, and the huge Christian book and music industries:

- Seven out of ten adults in the United States have no clue what "John 3:16" means.
- Only 31 percent know the meaning of the expression "the gospel."

—George Barna, *Evangelism That Works*

PERSONAL JOURNEY: TO DO ON YOUR OWN BETWEEN SESSIONS

During this session, you've been challenged to think about ways in which God can use you in your workplace. The following exercises will enhance your understanding and application of what you have discovered.

1. Read the following chart and consider the areas of common ground you already share with non-Christians. In which new activities are you willing to become involved in order to develop relationships with more non-Christians? Write down the names of several people with whom you want to find common ground and being building those relationships.

AREAS OF COMMON GROUND	OPTIONS TO CONSIDER	SPECIFIC PEOPLE AND ACTIVITIES
Interests	Spectator sports, outdoor recreation, competitive sports, reading, politics, bird watching, gardening, movies, gourmet foods, travel, cultural or historical interests, etc.	
Needs	Helping to meet needs such as offering a ride, helping someone move, fixing a computer, doing yardwork, repairing a car, babysitting, etc. Asking non-Christians for help—when someone invests in your life, he or she becomes interested in you.	
Gifts and Talents	Playing music, playing sports, doing drama, doing art together, etc.	
Location	Build on your location to nurture relationships: hike on a nearby trail, get to know someone you commute with, eat lunch with people from work, etc.	

cont.

| Common Concerns | Connect with parents about children's issues. Get involved in a school board or zoning issue with other neighbors. Go to public meetings together, join volunteer service organizations. | |

2. As we build relationships with non-Christians, we may encounter destructive, sinful behavior. It can be difficult to know how to respond to such behavior without building walls or compromising our commitments. The Scripture passages in the following chart will remind us of God's perspective on sin. Take time to read them, taking note of the perspective and reminder. Then ask God to open your heart and mind to how he wants you to conduct your relationships with non-Christians.

DEALING WITH THE REALITY OF SIN	
Scripture's Perspective	Helpful Reminder
We must not be surprised at people's sinfulness, thereby being self-righteous and hypocritical. See Romans 3:21–24; Jeremiah 17:9; Proverbs 20:9; 1 Peter 5:8–9.	We have all sinned and fallen short of God's glory. Not one of us is "immune" to sin. The hearts of all people are deceitful, and Satan still tries to entice Christians into committing sin.
Our job isn't to get non-Christians to conform to biblical behavior; it is to help them see their need for heart-level transformation. See John 16:5–9; 1 Corinthians 5:9–13.	Conviction of sin is the Holy Spirit's job, not ours. We are not called to separate ourselves from non-Christians who sin, but we are instructed to separate from Christians who practice evil.
We are to reach out to non-Christians but to avoid evil. Our reputation rests in God's hands. See 1 Thessalonians 5:22–24; Matthew 5:13–16; 9:10–13; 11:19; Romans 12:9; Ephesians 6:10–11.	Jesus befriended sinners. When we befriend sinners we will be exposed to evil, but we must continue to refrain from evil. God gives us his power to resist the devil's evil schemes.

We base our behavioral choices on biblical truth, not opinions. See Romans 14:1–5.	Sincere believers can differ on the amount of freedom they have in living as Christians. We are not to impose our convictions on someone else but to evaluate our standards by God's Word. When Scripture does not specify behavior, we should carefully make up our own minds without adding unbiblical rules to Christian living. When we need to say no to an activity, we are to do so with grace.

3. Commit to pray several minutes each day for the non-Christian coworkers and friends named on your common ground chart (pages 47–48). As you interact with each person, ask yourself, *What is God doing in this person's life, and what can I do to come alongside?* Then see what happens.

BE A WITNESS? OF COURSE YOU CAN!

Unless we show and tell what Jesus is doing in our lives, non-Christians will miss what Jesus can do for them. Unless they see joy in us as we work, unless they see the grace and peace Jesus gives us when we encounter difficult situations or ornery people, when we are disappointed or feel hurt or rejected, or when we get a bad diagnosis, they're not likely to get the message that Jesus can make a difference for them.

4. For further study on the topics covered in this session, read chapters 3 and 8 of the book *Workplace Grace* if you haven't done so already.

BEFORE SESSION 4

Please read chapter 4 of the book *Workplace Grace*.

EARNING THE RIGHT TO BE HEARD

If a person does not trust us, he or she will never trust what we say about Jesus.... Trust is *not* built on communication skills or evangelistic techniques.... It's a response to our competence, character, and actions. It must be earned.

BEFORE YOU BEGIN

Your experience in this session will be greatly enhanced by reading chapters 4 of the book *Workplace Grace*.

QUESTIONS TO THINK ABOUT

1. What kinds of resistance or emotional barriers against Christianity and Christians (indifference, mistrust, antagonism, anger, and fear, for example) have you encountered in your interactions with non-Christians? What do you think caused that response?

2. What do you think enables a Christian to have a positive spiritual influence in the workplace? Which specific attitudes and actions play a role in building trust?

VIDEO OUTLINE

Recognizing objections and emotional barriers

Overcoming barriers through relationships of trust

Five key traits:

    Professional competence

    Christlike character

    Thoughtful consideration

    Wise communication

    Courage to "become a distribution point of grace"

VIDEO DISCUSSION

1. Why is it important for us to examine our hearts before we try to talk about our faith at work?

2. What kinds of things do we Christians do that can cause non-Christians to put up emotional barriers against Christians and Christianity?

3. Bill and Walt argue that professional competence is the number-one requirement for earning the right to be heard in the workplace. Do you agree or disagree? If you disagree, what do you believe is the number-one requirement?

GROUP BIBLE EXPLORATION

TRUST-BUILDING TRAITS

If we are to build trust with non-Christians, we must earn it by our character and actions and win it through caring and meaningful relationships. Bill and Walt have identified five essential traits—competence, character, consideration, communication, and courage—that we must exhibit if we expect non-Christians to trust us enough to allow us to influence them. Let's explore the first three of these traits that pave the way for authentic communication.

BE A WITNESS? OF COURSE YOU CAN!

If we want people to pay attention to our faith, we must first pay attention to our work. Before we introduce coworkers to God, we must introduce God into our work.

---

1. Bill and Walt consider our professional excellence to be the foundational requirement for spiritual influence in the workplace.

    a. What does the Bible say about pursuing excellence in the workplace? (See Ecclesiastes 9:10; Proverbs 22:29; Colossians 3:23.)

    b. Just how dedicated and disciplined are we supposed to be in our pursuit of excellence? (See 1 Corinthians 9:25–27; Philippians 3:13–14.)

BE A WITNESS? OF COURSE YOU CAN!

When we exhibit love, joy, and peace, we are magnetic. Patience, kindness, goodness, faithfulness, gentleness, and self-control speak loudly that we are people who can be trusted. Even if people hate what we believe, over time they will be attracted to Jesus' character reflected in and overflowing from us.

2. The second trait that nurtures trust is Christlike character.

   a. Where does Christlike character come from? (See Galatians 5:22–25.)

   b. What does Christlike character accomplish in us? (See 2 Corinthians 3:18; Titus 2:12.)

   c. What is the result of having Christlike character? (See 1 Peter 2:11–12.)

BE A WITNESS? OF COURSE YOU CAN!

Nothing reveals more about your character than how you treat people.... Character expresses itself outwardly in the thoughtfulness we display to others—our tenderness and compassion, our mercy and kindness, our attentiveness and gentleness.

3. The third trait that builds trust is thoughtful consideration of other people.

   a. Scripture has much to say about how we are to treat people. What examples of consideration are highlighted in the following passages? (See Philippians 2:1–4; Ephesians 4:31–32; 1 Peter 4:10.)

   b. Thoughtful consideration isn't limited to our actions. The manner in which we communicate with others reveals much about how greatly we value them. In what ways does God want us to show consideration for others through our communication? (See Ephesians 4:29; James 1:19–20.)

SPIRITUAL INFLUENCE OPENS THE DOOR TO COMMUNICATION

Professional excellence, character, and daily consideration of others are essential if we are to become spiritually influential people. These traits, when displayed through caring relationships, cultivate the packed soil of hardened hearts and earn for us the right to be heard. That's right, "the right to be *heard*!" The next step in the evangelism process is to speak out about our faith when appropriate opportunities arise.

4. What does 1 Peter 3:15–16 reveal about wise communication?

5. What types of conversations should we, as Christians, be known for? (See Luke 6:45; Ephesians 4:29; Psalm 15:1–3.)

6. An important part of wise communication is discerning when it is (and is not) appropriate to talk about our faith. Read the following chart, then discuss with your group specific examples or applications to your workplace.

APPROPRIATE SITUATION	APPROPRIATE MESSAGE
When it arises out of relationships naturally built around your work.	As you discuss work and life, informal mention of spiritual truth will happen naturally, in the same way other topics come up.
When it fits naturally into the topic of conversation.	Our conversations about our faith should be natural, not contrived, crafted, or calculated to divert discussion into a totally unrelated area. Inappropriate comments can chill conversations as well as budding relationships.
When you are asked.	A question is an open door to address a person's spiritual concern, but it isn't an invitation to dump all of your spiritual knowledge at once! Answer the question and try to stimulate further questions that will keep the dialogue open. (For questions of legality, see Alliance Defense Fund's pamphlet, "The truth about Faith in the Workplace" at www.alliance defensefund.org/issues/religiousfreedom/intheworkplace.aspx?cid=3167.)

7. We often are our own worst enemies when it comes to earning the right to be heard.

   a. What kinds of things should we avoid doing or saying because they may cause non-Christians to put up barriers toward Christians and Christianity?

   b. What can we do to counteract the damage done by these words and actions?

A NOTE OF CAUTION

Entrepreneur Anne Beiler reminds us how essential authentic communication is for Christians in the workplace: "If your light is going to shine, your actions should confirm what you say. If your actions don't confirm what you say, then you confuse those around you."

---

8. What impact does hypocrisy on the part of Christians have on the hearts of non-Christians? Why is hypocrisy so damaging to the cause of Christ?

9. In your relationships with non-Christians in the workplace, have you tended to focus more on the heart or the head? What specific adjustments in attitude might you make in order to have greater spiritual influence?

PERSONAL JOURNEY: TO DO ON YOUR OWN BETWEEN SESSIONS

During this session, you've been challenged to think about ways in which God can use you in your workplace. The following exercises will enhance your understanding and application of what you have discovered during this session.

1. As you interact with people this week, pay close attention to your listening skills. If they are less than perfect (and most of us fit into this category), begin working at becoming a better listener.

2. Continue to look for relationship-building opportunities with non-Christians in your workplace. Ask God to help you develop the five essential traits for a positive spiritual influence and to guide you to people who need to experience his love.

3. For further study on the topics covered in this session, read chapter 4 of the book *Workplace Grace* if you haven't done so already.

BEFORE SESSION 5

Please read chapters 5, 6, 9, and 11 of the book *Workplace Grace*.

KEEP IT SIMPLE: FROM CULTIVATING TO PLANTING

Planting involves far more than a onetime walk through the facts of the gospel. It entails helping a person address sincere, well-founded, and perhaps long-standing intellectual questions about faith issues.... More and more people ... need both good information and nonthreatening ways to investigate what the Bible says about who they are, who Jesus is, and what he has done for them.

BEFORE YOU BEGIN

Your experience in this session will be greatly enhanced by reading chapters 5, 6, 9, and 11 of the book *Workplace Grace*.

QUESTIONS TO THINK ABOUT

1. What acts of kindness have people done for you? When someone goes out of his or her way to do something kind for you, how do you feel? How long do you remember it?

2. When talking with a person who disagrees with your point of view, what makes it possible to continue your discussion without it becoming an argument? What responses or attitudes tend to make you angry or lead you to want to end the conversation?

VIDEO OUTLINE

Witnessing or being a witness?

People want to be friends, not projects

Faith flags

Faith stories

Objections—opportunity or obstacle?

VIDEO DISCUSSION

1. What is the difference between "witnessing" and being a "witness," and why should it matter to us?

BE A WITNESS? OF COURSE YOU CAN!

People want to see the truth *pictured* in our lives. That's why *faith flags* and *faith stories* are such powerful ways to communicate spiritual truth and create curiosity.

---

2. What is a *faith flag*, and how does it work?

3. What is a *faith story*, and how does it work?

4. We'll examine in greater detail how to handle objections to Christianity later in this session, but what did you learn from the video about the role of objections in the evangelism process and how to respond to them?

GROUP BIBLE EXPLORATION

WHAT KIND OF A WITNESS?

Many Christians have never understood the difference between being a
witness and *witnessing*. The confusion has caused many of us to believe
we can't be persons of spiritual influence anywhere, much less in the workplace. But the Bible reveals that each of us can be an effective witness. Bill
and Walt describe our role as witnesses very simply: "We are called to *be*
witnesses—to show and tell what we have seen and what we know. We are
to be witnesses of the way that God, through faith, prayer, and the Bible,
has transformed our lives."

1. We can offer two kinds of witness. As *material* witnesses, we give an
    account of what God has done for us—what we have seen, heard,
    and experienced in our daily lives. As *expert* witnesses, we explain
    and sometimes defend the facts and credibility of Christianity. The
    Bible includes examples of both types of witness, but we will focus
    our attention on being a *material* witness. Read John 9:1, 6–15,
    24–27 and answer the following questions.

    a. What kind of witness—material or expert—was the blind man
        Jesus healed?

    b. What kind of witness did the Pharisees pressure him to be? (See
        vv. 24–27.)

2. After Jesus healed the demoniac, what kind of witness did Jesus
    ask him to be? What impact did the man have? (See Mark 5:1–5,
    11–20.)

BE A WITNESS? OF COURSE YOU CAN!

The Bible clearly teaches that true love is love in action. Common courtesies can be the most basic way we show love in action. We don't need a theological education or know all the answers or have great giftedness. But it does take determination to show the love of Jesus to people around us.

3. One of the amazing things about being a "witness" rather than "witnessing" is that it is something we can be in every one of the "divine appointments" God gives us with non-Christians every day. Each encounter is an opportunity to build upon a relationship of trust, an opportunity to express Christian love in action, and may be an open door to further spiritual curiosity or conversation. The key to being a witness is to let the love and grace of God shine through us in our everyday actions.

    John 6:5–14 gives us an idea of what God can do when we respond to the kinds of opportunities to be a witness that open up before us every day. What happened in this story, and what does it reveal about how God can work through everyday acts of kindness?

TURNING OBJECTIONS INTO OPPORTUNITIES

As people move closer to a personal relationship with God, their resistance to Christianity often increases. Not only may the enemy of their souls be sensing defeat, they may have misconceptions and long-standing questions or concerns about Christianity. So planting is not just a quick walk through the facts of the gospel. Thoughtful, gracious conversation about biblical truth within the context of a meaningful relationship can address objections related to sincere faith issues.

4. We are sometimes tempted to minimize the importance of intellectual objections to Christianity and encourage people to "just believe." Read the following Scripture passages and note why it is important to address intellectual questions.

Scripture	The Value of Intellectual Questions
Proverbs 18:15, 17	
Romans 12:2	
2 Corinthians 4:1–4	

5. Some objections to Christianity are best handled by sharing biblical truth, but some ways of sharing are better than others. Bill and Walt give us three key principles for lovingly sharing biblical truth that will help us handle objections in such a way that they become opportunities, not obstacles. Read each principle and Scripture passage, then explain why the principle is effective.

a. Use the Bible whenever you can. (See Hebrews 4:12.)

b. Balance truth with grace. (See John 8:10–11.)

c. Balance knowledge with humility. (See 1 Corinthians 8:1–3.)

6. It's easy for us to develop "insider" vocabulary that makes no sense to or even offends non-Christians. Although biblical, terminology as common as "washed in the blood," "lost," or "born again" may be incomprehensible, provoke anger, or bring up impressions that kill spiritual curiosity. So why use them and risk offending the person you are talking to? Choose several of the following terms and come up with other words that convey the meaning of these concepts:

redeemed	saved
lost	ask Jesus into your heart
sin	obey God's laws
born again	the gospel

BE A WITNESS? OF COURSE YOU CAN!

Learning how to ask nonthreatening questions is one of the Christian's best tools for dealing with objections. Questions communicate interest and humility and allow people to discover truth for themselves. Although a simple answer to a direct question is often the best response, answering a question with a question can encourage further dialogue. Jason Dulle suggests using three types of questions:

• *Questions of clarification:* "What do you mean by that?"

These help us understand the underlying concerns and challenge people to express clearly what they want to say.

• *Questions of justification:* "How did you arrive at that conclusion?"

These uncover what people believe and allow us to see the logic behind their beliefs.

• *Questions of consideration:* "Have you ever considered ...?"

These can give us opportunities to introduce new information or points of view in nonthreatening ways.

—Jason Dulle, *"The Question of Truth and Apologetics in a Postmodern World"*

7. When we talk with people who hold views that don't conform to the truth of Scripture, we will encounter objections. Because it's important for us to handle these objections in love, let's consider ways to express disagreement while maintaining respect, gentleness, and thoughtfulness. What we say and how we say it can keep the door open for future discussion or cause it to slam shut.

    As a group, discuss the following phrases you may have used in the past and consider the suggested alternatives, or come up with other options. Talk about the results of using some of these phrases. Did they lead to obstacles or opportunities? If you feel comfortable doing so, share how you would like a similar discussion to be different next time.

PHRASES TO AVOID	PHRASES TO CONSIDER USING
It's a proven fact that …	Correct me if I'm wrong, but I see a conflict between …
You don't know what you're talking about.	I'm not piecing the facts together in the same way.
Well, if you believe that, then …	Have you considered the evidence for …?
You're totally illogical.	My perspective is a little different. May I share it with you?
How can you even say that?	I hear what you are saying, but it does raise a red flag for me.
Look at the evidence.	Can I offer you another opinion?
You're not serious!	I was wondering, have you ever considered …?
There's no question about …	I agree with you concerning _____, but I see the issue differently.
Give me a break. That has been totally disproved.	I'm not sure I agree. Could I hear that again?

— "Heart for the Harvest" seminar manual, Search Ministries

8. What specific things did you learn in this discussion that will help you deal more lovingly and effectively with a person's objections to the Christian faith?

JUST A REMINDER: WHAT IS A FAITH FLAG?

- A brief statement, told in the natural course of a conversation, that helps identify us as people to whom faith, the Bible, prayer, and God are important
- Creates an opportunity for people to ask us about our faith
- Looks for, but doesn't demand, a response
- Provides a nonthreatening way to gauge people's spiritual interest and discover what God is doing in their lives

---

9. Many people today relate to personal stories that speak to the emotions and seize the imagination. Personal stories of our experiences with God give people tangible, authentic views of God. Because people want to see the truth *pictured* in our lives, *faith flags* and *faith stories* are powerful ways to communicate spiritual truth and create curiosity.

   a. How would you describe a faith flag? Share some examples of how to use one effectively.

b. How would you describe a faith story? Share some examples of how to use one effectively.

JUST A REMINDER: WHAT IS A FAITH STORY?

- A one- to two-minute testimony about a specific time when something spiritual happened to us—showing that God is at work and making a difference in our lives
- Portrays in narrative form how God, the Bible, and/or prayer have been real or meaningful to us
- Should be a natural part of the conversation, not something artificially dropped into it
- Explains *why* there's something attractive about us, about the God who is at work in us
- Allows us to link our personal stories to specific needs in people's lives

Personal Journey: To Do on Your Own Between Sessions

During this session, you've been challenged to think about ways in which God can use you to extend his grace in your workplace. The following exercises will enhance your understanding and application of what you have discovered.

1. Write down the names of at least three non-Christians with whom you have relationships in the workplace. For each one, first consider where that person is in his or her spiritual journey, then consider your relationship with that person and ways you might be able to come alongside to be a more effective spiritual influence. The questions in the following chart will help you think of specific things you can do.

Evaluation Point	Person 1	Person 2	Person 3
Which phase of evangelism best represents where this person is today—cultivating, planting, or harvesting?			
What kind of witness do you tend to be with this person—material or expert?			
How authentic is your witness with this person? On which area(s) do you need to work?			
Which common courtesies or acts of kindness are most meaningful to this person?			

EVALUATION POINT	PERSON 1	PERSON 2	PERSON 3
Which spiritual objections or obstacles have you encountered with this person?			
How well did you handle those objections at the time? What improvements do you want to make?			
Based on your knowledge of this person, think of several *faith flags* or *faith stories* that you think will connect.			
What specifically will you pray for in relationship to this person's spiritual journey?			

2. Read Acts 26 and answer the following questions about the "faith story" Paul told as he stood before King Agrippa and his court.

   a. How did Paul introduce his story? (See vv. 2–3.)

   b. What did Paul then tell about himself? (See vv. 4–11.)

c. What did Paul describe in verses 12–18?

d. How did Paul close his "faith story"? (See vv. 19–22a.)

e. Why was Paul's "faith story" so powerful? (See vv. 27–29.)

3. Set aside time this week to develop one or two of your own faith stories. Telling specific, personal stories of how you came to know Jesus or how knowing him has enriched your life is a compelling way to convey spiritual truth to coworkers and friends.

The following steps will help you know what to include in your faith stories:

Step one: List times when you have had meaningful encounters with God, such as:

• When God did something meaningful or significant in your life

• When you enjoyed and experienced pleasure in your relationship with God

- When God spoke clearly to you or gave you guidance

- When a particular passage of Scripture helped you on the job

- When God worked through you to accomplish his purposes

- When God answered a specific prayer

Step two: Choose one or two of these experiences and on a separate piece of paper write a brief faith story about each. Then keep these experiences in mind to use naturally in conversations with coworkers and friends.

BE A WITNESS? OF COURSE YOU CAN!

A faith story is not complicated or perfectly polished; it is simply a story about what God has done or is doing in your life. The following tips will help your story communicate clearly and personally:

- Use easy-to-listen-to conversational language. You're not writing a term paper.
- Tell a nonpreachy story about yourself. You're not telling about "them."
- Reveal general details — no specific names of people, churches, dates, denominations, etc.
- Reflect real-life experiences in a warm, pleasant, relaxed manner. Human interest or a humorous touch that makes listeners smile or laugh lowers their defenses.
- Create word pictures that make situations come alive in listeners' minds.
- Include a natural, nonthreatening "bridge" from your story to a brief explanation of the gospel.
- Show how God is meeting your deepest inner needs.

4. For further study on the topics covered in this session, read chapters 5, 6, 9, and 11 of the book *Workplace Grace* if you haven't done so already.

BEFORE SESSION 6

Please read chapters 10, 12, 13, and 14 of the book *Workplace Grace*.

FROM PLANTING TO HARVESTING

The work we call "planting" occurs when the seed of biblical truth is spread in love and with compassion to hearts that, because they have been cultivated, are receptive.

BEFORE YOU BEGIN

Your experience in this session will be greatly enhanced by reading chapters 10, 12, 13, and 14 of the book *Workplace Grace*.

QUESTIONS TO THINK ABOUT

1. How do you recognize whether the minds of your coworkers and friends are open or shut to spiritual discussion, particularly about Jesus or the Bible? Which indicators of spiritual interest get your attention?

2. When you are discussing serious spiritual matters with a non-Christian, do you tend to be a talker or a listener? How does your normal behavior impact those discussions, and what might you want to change?

VIDEO OUTLINE

Recognizing and using "open doors"

Clearly presenting the gospel message

The joy of the harvest

VIDEO DISCUSSION

1. Why is it important for us to allow God to open spiritual doors for us rather than trying to open those doors on our own?

2. In what ways was the gospel presentation shown in the video clear? Nonthreatening? Convincing? Inviting? Concise?

3. What did you learn from Bill's story or the dramatization that will help you to better explain the gospel to others?

4. Bill and Walt emphasized the importance of caring for new Christians so that they receive the love, training, and discipline necessary to mature in their faith. What are some ways we can help new Christians grow?

GROUP BIBLE EXPLORATION

EXPLAINING THE BASICS OF THE GOSPEL

As important as it is that people see the gospel lived out in the lives of Christians, at an appropriate time the gospel message must be explained to them if they are to believe in Jesus and receive eternal life. This explanation is particularly important in our day because a growing percentage of non-Christians don't know the basics of the gospel message. So being a spiritually influential person requires that we know how to present the gospel message clearly and concisely. Let's highlight the elements of a gospel presentation.

1. Known for his tireless presentation of the gospel, the apostle Paul had a fruitful witness nearly everywhere he went. In Colossians 4:3–4, he asked other believers to pray specifically for his presentation of the gospel. What did he request, and why is his request significant?

2. Why is it necessary to explain the gospel? (See Romans 10:14–17.)

3. What is the important message from God we are to share with people when the time is right? (See 1 Corinthians 15:1–6.)

4. What did Jesus do for us? (See Romans 5:8; Colossians 1:19–20; 1 Peter 3:18, 22.)

5. How do we receive the gift of eternal life from God? (See John 1:12–14; 3:16–18; Acts 16:31; Romans 3:22–26.)

6. In Matthew 22:17–20 and John 10:25–26, 36, how did Jesus respond to the questions asked of him? How can this approach help in our discussions of spiritual matters with non-Christians?

7. As important as cultivating and planting are, what do John 4:35–38
   and Luke 15:3–7 reveal about spiritual harvest?

THE GOSPEL IN A VERSE!

Romans 6:23 summarizes the key message of all sixty-six books
of the Bible: "For the wages of sin is death, but the gift of God is
eternal life in Christ Jesus our Lord."

Some of the terms used in this verse may be unfamiliar, confusing, or obstacles to non-Christians, so here are some suggestions
for explaining them.

SIN: *Sin* literally means "to fall short, to miss the mark," so sin
is falling short of God's standards. It's not about obeying religious
rules; it's about an improper relationship with the Creator of the
universe. None of us have met God's standard; we all have sinned.
(See Isaiah 53:6; Romans 5:6–17; 6:8–14.)

DEATH: The word *death* refers not just to physical death (separation from the body) but to spiritual death (eternal separation
from God, who is the source of life). Physical death is a result of
spiritual death. The wages of sin result in separation from God.
(See Psalm 68:20; 1 Corinthians 15:50–57; 2 Timothy 1:8–10;
Hebrews 2:14–15; 1 Peter 1:24.)

GIFT: God has given us a free gift with no strings attached—
eternal life. But we have to receive that gift by admitting our sin
and choosing to begin a personal relationship with God. This relationship, made possible by Jesus' death on the cross and his res-
urrection, meets our deepest longings. (See John 3:14–18; 11:25;
Ephesians 1:7; 2:8–9; 1 Peter 1:18–19.)

MINIMUM DAILY REQUIREMENTS FOR NEW BELIEVERS' SPIRITUAL GROWTH

Just as parents are responsible to nurture and care for their newborn child, those of us who are involved in spiritual harvesting have a responsibility to see that new believers receive spiritual care after they accept God's gift of salvation. Jesus' last instructions to his disciples indicated that they were to make disciples, not just believers (Matthew 28:19–20), so let's consider our role in a new believer's life and what kind of "spiritual diet" new Christians need.

BE A WITNESS? OF COURSE YOU CAN!

When you discover that the hearts of several coworkers and/or friends have been cultivated to the point that they want to receive more biblical truth, consider starting a Bible study. It's an effective way to help non-Christians discover biblical truth for themselves in a supportive atmosphere. You don't have to be a Bible scholar to lead it, just a fellow traveler on the same road of discovering more about who Jesus is and what God is teaching in his Word. The Bible is powerful, and God will speak through it to anyone who comes with a seeker's heart.

---

8. Acts 2:42–47 describes five core experiences (much like five minimum daily requirements in a healthy diet) that all believers — especially new believers — need in their spiritual diet. What are they?

   a. Verse 42 (See also John 8:31–32; Psalm 1:1–2; 2 Timothy 3:16–17; James 1:22–25.)

   b. Verses 44–45 (See also Galatians 5:13–14; 1 Peter 4:8–11.)

c. Verses 46–47 (See also John 4:23–24; Hebrews 12:28; Psalm 95:6–7.)

d. Verses 44–46 (See also Romans 15:5–7; Ephesians 4:2–6; Colossians 3:13–16.)

e. Verse 47 (See also Matthew 28:19–20; Romans 1:16; Ephesians 3:8–12.)

SPIRITUAL GROWTH IS A PROCESS

All of us need a growing understanding of who God has made us to be in Jesus Christ. Depending on the type of baggage they still carry, new Christians will need different kinds of help. Some will need skillful, Bible-based counseling and healing prayer to unplug the power of past pain and hurt before they can experience God's power. Some will need correction and the assurance of our love and God's love. Some will need to learn to overcome negative self-talk. Some will need help with fear, guilt, or lack of trust in God. Some will need a nudge, or even a shove, to wake them up to the reality of what they are doing to others and themselves.

9. Take a few minutes and together review the chart below that outlines the seven basic questions a gospel presentation should answer.

SEVEN BASIC QUESTIONS A GOSPEL PRESENTATION SHOULD ANSWER	
1. Who is God?	God is a personal, eternal, all-powerful, all-knowing, ever-present, supremely great spiritual being. He created the heavens and earth and is the source of meaning, life, and love. He has revealed himself as one, true, eternal God in three persons (the Trinity)—Father, Son, and Holy Spirit.
2. Who are we?	Created by God to rule the world and live in perfect relationship with him and one another, we rebelled and chose to please ourselves rather than to follow God. As a result, we plunged the world into pain, insecurity, confusion, and powerlessness. Having disobeyed in actions and attitudes, we missed God's mark and can't live up to our own standards, much less God's. So we are separated from God and under judgment, unable to escape the bondage of wrongdoing.
3. Who is Jesus?	Jesus is the eternal, divine Son of God, Lord of the universe. He loves humankind so much that he left heaven for earth—to live, die, be resurrected, and thus restore his original purpose for us.
4. What did Jesus do?	Jesus did for us what we couldn't do for ourselves. He chose to take our judgment and die in our place. Because he is truly God and was also truly human and truly righteous, he could take the penalty of our sin—the sentence of death—on himself. In so doing, he made forgiveness, a relationship with God, and eternal life possible. His life restores our lives.
5. What can we not do?	We can't change the way we are, earn our pardon, or free ourselves from the sentence of death by our good deeds, faith plus good deeds, or faith plus good intentions.
6. What do we have to do?	All we have to do is the only thing we can do—receive Jesus, God's eternal Son, as our own Savior by faith, depending totally on him as the only basis for our relationship with God.
7. What does God promise to those who believe?	He promises to forgive all our wrongdoing, give us eternal life, make us part of his family, make his home in our hearts, and love us unconditionally. He will strengthen us as we face our problems and grants us the power to become everything we were designed to be, living lives overflowing with meaning and purpose.

Do you have any questions about these points? Is there anything about them that you find confusing? Which additions would you make to this outline? Which Scripture passages would you use to explain these points?

PERSONAL JOURNEY: TO DO ON YOUR OWN IN THE COMING DAYS

1. Carefully read the "Principles of Walking Through an Opening Spiritual Door" below and on page 91, and consider how you might respond when you begin to hear the squeak of an opening door in the future. Evaluate how well you've used these principles during previous discussions with non-Christians, and note how you can use these principles more effectively in the future.

PRINCIPLES OF WALKING THROUGH AN OPENING SPIRITUAL DOOR			
Principle	Suggestions	Past Experience	Future Ideas
Proceed slowly.	Listen to the Holy Spirit's whisper rather than rushing in to give advice, share scriptural principles, or fix things		
Ask permission to speak further.	Ask, "May I share something I've learned about that?" or "May I tell you a story about some help I got with a similar problem?" With permission, we can share faith stories with little risk of rejection.		
Be sensitive to your listener(s).	Watch for verbal and nonverbal cues that the spiritual door remains open or is beginning to close. Be careful about using religious jargon, and don't abuse company time. If necessary, schedule a time to talk after work.		

Check regularly to see if your listener(s) is still with you.	Ask, ask, ask, and then listen. Most planting involves dialogue — not preaching or teaching. Avoid one-way conversations.		
Regulate the dosage.	Take one step at a time. Intrigue people with a little truth rather than overwhelming them with more than they can process. Leave the results to God, and let the Holy Spirit set the schedule.		
Don't react negatively to objections.	Recognize the role that doubt can play in a person's life. Emotional obstacles (such as anger and hostility) may resurface during the planting stage, even in a relationship of trust. Don't take these emotions personally.		

2. God wants each of us to use our gifts and talents to help "baby" Christians become more mature in their faith. When you meet a new Christian who is not yet being discipled, ask yourself the following questions — then act!

   • What do I have that can contribute to this person's spiritual growth?

   • What specific things could I teach this person?

   • How much time do I have available to spend with him or her?

- With which other concerned Christians does this person already have a relationship?

- To what other caring Christians can I introduce this person?

- What other resources are needed for this person's spiritual growth?

- Which books or resources that I've read would help this person grow spiritually?

- Which church(es) would most help this person?

- What kind of gifts could this person bring to the body of Christ?

3. For further study on the topics covered in this session, read chapters 10, 12, 13, and 14 of the book *Workplace Grace* if you haven't done so already.

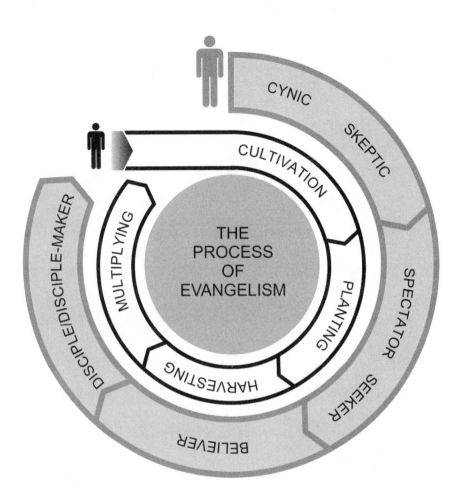

THE PROCESS OF EVANGELISM

CYNIC
SKEPTIC
SPECTATOR
SEEKER
BELIEVER
DISCIPLE/DISCIPLE-MAKER

CULTIVATION
PLANTING
HARVESTING
MULTIPLYING

Workplace Grace

Becoming a Spiritual Influence at Work

Bill Peel and Walt Larimore

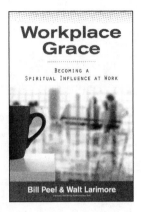

How to take evangelism out of the religious box and weave it into your life at work

In every part of the world, people are looking for spiritual answers and resources as never before. But you don't need to travel to some exotic foreign mission field to find hungry hearts. You spend hours every day in the most strategic place of impact in the world—your workplace.

Workplace Grace, formerly titled *Going Public with Your Faith*—winner of the EPCA Silver Medallion and Christianity Today Book Awards, offers a proven model for evangelism that respects the unique relationships you have with your coworkers, clients, or customers. It shows how you can be authentic instead of artificial when sharing what you believe, build trust with even the most skeptical person, and cultivate caring connections with those who have not yet come to a saving faith in Christ.

Available in stores and online!

Share Your Thoughts

With the Author: Your comments will be forwarded to the author when you send them to *zauthor@zondervan.com*.

With Zondervan: Submit your review of this book by writing to *zreview@zondervan.com*.

Free Online Resources at
www.zondervan.com

Zondervan AuthorTracker: Be notified whenever your favorite authors publish new books, go on tour, or post an update about what's happening in their lives at www.zondervan.com/authortracker.

Daily Bible Verses and Devotions: Enrich your life with daily Bible verses or devotions that help you start every morning focused on God. Visit www.zondervan.com/newsletters.

Free Email Publications: Sign up for newsletters on Christian living, academic resources, church ministry, fiction, children's resources, and more. Visit www.zondervan.com/newsletters.

Zondervan Bible Search: Find and compare Bible passages in a variety of translations at www.zondervanbiblesearch.com.

Other Benefits: Register yourself to receive online benefits like coupons and special offers, or to participate in research.

ZONDERVAN®

ZONDERVAN.com/
AUTHORTRACKER
follow your favorite authors